The Library of
ASTRONAUT BIOGRAPHIES™

JAMES LOVELL

The Rescue of *Apollo 13*

Jan Goldberg

The Rosen Publishing Group, Inc., New York

Published in 2004 by The Rosen Publishing Group, Inc.
29 East 21st Street, New York, NY 10010

Library of Congress Cataloging-in-Publication Data

Goldberg, Jan.
James Lovell: the rescue of *Apollo 13*/Jan Goldberg.—1st ed.
    p. cm.—(The library of astronaut biographies)
Summary: A biography of James Lovell that encompasses the astronaut's
birth, childhood, education, NASA training, mission experience, and
post-space life and work.
Includes bibliographical references and index.
ISBN 0-8239-4459-X (library binding)
1. Lovell, Jim—Juvenile literature. 2. Astronauts—United States—
Biography—Juvenile literature. 3. *Apollo 13* (Spacecraft)—Accidents—
Juvenile literature. 4. Space vehicle accidents—United States—Juvenile
literature. [1. Lovell, Jim. 2. Astronauts. 3. *Apollo 13* (Spacecraft) 4. Space
vehicle accidents.] I. Title. II. Series.
TL789.85.L68G65 2004
629.45'0092—dc22

                                                        2003014303

Manufactured in the United States of America

CONTENTS

INTRODUCTION	The Far Side of the Moon	4
CHAPTER 1	Racing to Space	8
CHAPTER 2	Lovell's First Trip to Space	25
CHAPTER 3	*Gemini 12*	44
CHAPTER 4	*Apollo 8* and the Giant Leap	53
CHAPTER 5	The Rescue of *Apollo 13*	75
CONCLUSION	A Down-to-Earth Hero	97
GLOSSARY		103
FOR MORE INFORMATION		105
FOR FURTHER READING		107
BIBLIOGRAPHY		108
INDEX		110

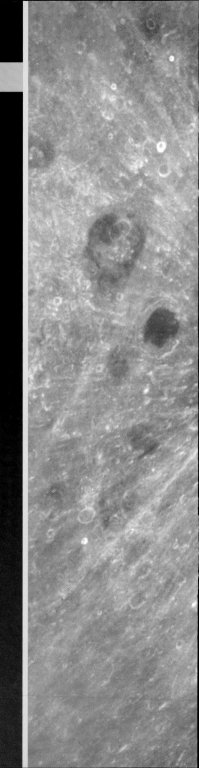

THE FAR SIDE OF THE MOON

Though his name is not among the most imme-diately recognizable of the early NASA astronauts, James Lovell managed to quietly rack up a long list of pioneering accomplishments during his long and successful career in the space program. He was the first astronaut in history to fly four missions in space. He was the first astronaut to fly to the Moon twice. In 1965, he set the record for the longest manned space-flight aboard *Gemini* 7. During

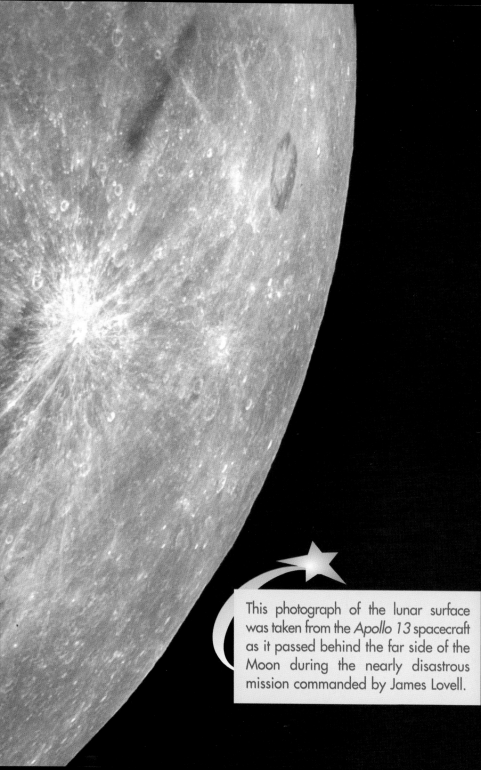

This photograph of the lunar surface was taken from the *Apollo 13* spacecraft as it passed behind the far side of the Moon during the nearly disastrous mission commanded by James Lovell.

that same mission, he participated in the first rendezvous (close approach) of two manned spacecraft. During the *Apollo 8* mission alone, he and his fellow crew members earned three "firsts": first humans to travel beyond Earth's orbit, first astronauts to orbit the Moon, and the first human beings ever to see the far side of the Moon with their own eyes.

Despite this long and distinguished record of groundbreaking achievement, James Lovell is most often remembered as the man who did not land on the Moon. As commander of the ill-fated *Apollo 13*, Lovell kept a cool head and a brave heart and calmly managed a crisis that threatened to spiral out of control. The odds were against him and his crew. Without quick thinking, expert problem solving, and grace under pressure, *Apollo 13* was destined to be lost in space forever, 200,000 miles (321,869 kilometers) away from Lovell's home on Earth. Together, he, his crew, and the NASA engineers and flight controllers on the ground avoided this likely disaster.

James Lovell may be remembered as the man who did not land on the Moon. In this case, however, just getting home was a triumph and achievement far more difficult, demanding, and heroic than any Moon landing. Even though the mission he commanded was a failure in almost all respects and achieved none of its important goals, *Apollo 13* was one of NASA's shining moments. It was second only to the first Moon landing of *Apollo 11*, its greatest triumph.

James Lovell was the hero at the center of this gripping real-life drama. He may have lost the opportunity to walk on the lunar surface, but he gained the far greater honor of rescuing *Apollo 13* from the dark side of the Moon.

CHAPTER 1

RACING TO SPACE

J ames A. Lovell Jr. was born in Cleveland, Ohio, on March 25, 1928. He and his parents, Blanche and James A. Lovell Sr., soon moved to Milwaukee, Wisconsin. The man who would one day become one of the United States's most famous astronauts first turned his gaze toward the stars in high school. In 1944, at the age of sixteen, Lovell and some friends, assisted by their chemistry teacher, worked hard to build a primitive, or very simple, rocket. The rocket was powered by airplane glue and gunpowder. Liftoff was promising, as the rocket shot up 80 feet (24 meters) into the air. It

James Lovell was born in Cleveland, Ohio, in 1928. The one-year-old Lovell is pictured in the inset. The Lovells soon moved to Milwaukee, Wisconsin, where James grew up and attended high school. He is seen here at the age of twelve, standing with his bike outside the family home.

quickly began to wobble, however, and suddenly exploded. This brief, failed flight, modest as it was, provided the spark of hope and imagination that, once ignited, would one day carry James Lovell to the Moon.

Rocket Studies

Lovell graduated from Milwaukee's Solomon Juneau High School in 1946. Far from being discouraged by the failure of his first rocket launch, Lovell hoped to

While attending Solomon Juneau High School in Milwaukee, Wisconsin, James Lovell also worked in the school's cafeteria. He is seen here serving up lunch for his classmates. Lovell's work ethic and can-do spirit would one day carry him far off from Milwaukee, all the way to the Moon.

pursue rocket science and aeronautics (the science of flight) in college. Unfortunately, no colleges offered a degree in rocket science yet. Lovell realized that the only way he could gain the knowledge he desired was through the military. As a result, he applied to the United States Naval Academy in Annapolis, Maryland. More disappointment followed. Rather than being accepted right away, Lovell was put on a waiting list. His dream of flight would have to be put on hold for a few years.

Wanting to put his time to good use, Lovell decided to enroll in college to begin gaining the science foundation he would need if he wanted to become a top pilot and aeronautical engineer. He enrolled at the University of Wisconsin, where he found a way to keep his dreams of rocket flight alive while pursuing his studies—he took flying lessons. In 1948, however, only two years into his studies, Lovell would receive the break for which he had been hoping—he was accepted into the U.S. Naval Academy. His civilian college days had suddenly come to an end. James Lovell was in the navy now!

This is a yearbook portrait of James Lovell from 1952, the year he graduated from the U.S. Naval Academy with a bachelor of science degree.

Naval Aviation

Soon after graduating from the U.S. Naval Academy in 1952, Lovell attended the Naval Air Training Station in Pensacola, Florida, for flight training. After fourteen months of training, he was assigned to Moffet Field, in Mountain View, California. He did not have to travel west alone, however. On the same day Lovell graduated from the U.S. Naval Academy, he married his high school sweetheart, Marilyn Gerlach. They would have four children together—Barbara, James, Susan, and Jeffrey.

In California, Lovell was an officer in Composite Squadron Three, which specialized in all-weather flights from the aircraft carrier USS *Shangri-La*, stationed in the Pacific Ocean off the coast of Japan. Lovell mastered the special and demanding skills necessary for a naval aviator, including nighttime carrier landings. During one mission in which the lights on his instrument panel blinked out, he even had to land on the *Shangri-La*'s deck without being able to read his instruments at all. He was flying blind! His instincts and talent carried him through, however, to a safe landing.

This photograph captures the maiden flight on May 27, 1958, of the U.S. Navy's F4H Phantom jet fighter, which was designed to fly at twice the speed of sound. James Lovell served as the program manager for the Phantom from 1958 to 1962.

FROM SEA TO SKY

The U.S. Naval Academy is a four-year university in which graduates earn not only a diploma but also an officer's rank in the navy. Lovell completed his undergraduate degree in 1952, earning a bachelor of science degree. His early interest in rocketry had only increased with the passage of time, and the U.S. Naval Academy had allowed him to pursue it to a degree that no other university could. His senior thesis was on liquid fuel rocketry, a groundbreaking topic in 1952. Upon graduation, he was one of only fifty students—out of a class of 753—to be selected for training in naval aviation. Lovell would no longer have to stand on the earth gazing with longing at the sky above. He was about to take wing!

In 1957, these same piloting instincts and skills would carry him back east, to test pilot school at the Naval Air Test Center in Patuxent River, Maryland. Lovell graduated from test pilot school in 1958 and became a full-fledged test pilot and flight instructor for the U.S. Navy. During the four years he spent at Patuxent River as a test pilot, from 1958 to 1962, he served as program manager for the F4H Phantom fighter. First flown in May 1958, this fighter jet would remain in production until 1979 and become the backbone of the U.S. Navy's, Marine's, and Air Force's fighter fleets. Lovell also served as safety engineer for Fighter Squadron 101 at the Naval Air Station in Oceana, Virginia.

During his service as a test pilot and flight instructor, Lovell logged more than 5,000 hours flying time, 3,500 of them in jet aircraft. All of this time, effort, and expertise would soon be rewarded, however. James Lovell was about to be offered an opportunity to fly faster, farther, and higher than anyone had ever flown before. His youthful dream of rocket flight was about to come true.

The Cold War and the Space Race

Though World War II had come to an end in 1945, the postwar years remained a time of extreme global tension. The United States and the Soviet Union (modern-day Russia and other newly independent former Soviet republics)— once allies—began entering into a political and military struggle that affected nearly every other nation in the world. The United States believed in democracy and capitalism, in which people are free to elect their own government and buy and sell goods with little government control. The Soviet Union believed in Communism, which saw government's role as imposing equality on all its people, partly by controlling the flow of money so that extremes of wealth and poverty would no longer exist. Both nations wished to export their philosophies to other countries and create a world of like-minded nations.

In order to fight each other's international efforts, both nations began building and collecting large stockpiles of weapons, including nuclear

The successful launch of the Soviet satellite *Sputnik 1* created a worldwide sensation that mixed both fear and curiosity. In this 1957 photograph, a man gazes at a model of *Sputnik 1* displayed in the window of a department store in Rome, Italy.

bombs and missiles. A tense military standoff known as the Cold War ("cold" because the standoff never resulted in actual military combat between the superpowers) developed between the two superpowers and their various allies.

The Cold War stakes were raised on October 4, 1957, when the Soviet Union managed to

launch its first satellite, *Sputnik 1*, into space. *Sputnik 1* was only a tiny, 184-pound (83-kilogram) metallic ball that circled the Earth and emitted some harmless electronic beeps, but it struck fear in the hearts of many Americans. The successful launch of an artificial satellite beyond Earth's atmosphere and into orbit seemed to point toward a future in which the Soviets could strike the United States from land, sea, air, and now space. The Soviets could soon rule over space, fill it with weapons satellites, and dominate the free world from this new high ground.

The United States, which still had not successfully launched a rocket much less a satellite, had to catch up quickly if it hoped to keep pace with the Soviet Union, retain its global influence, and protect its national security. The space race was on.

The Birth of NASA

With the Soviets already in space, American scientists started to push for the creation of a government agency that would oversee the space program in the United States. United States president Dwight D. Eisenhower agreed with their arguments. On April 2, 1958, he submitted a space bill to Congress. The bill was soon passed, and Eisenhower signed the act—P. L. 58-568, the National Aeronautics and Space Act of 1958—on July 29. The National Aeronautics and Space Administration (NASA) was created as a result of the act. It was to be a civilian (nonmilitary) government agency committed to manned spaceflight and exploration. NASA opened its doors on October 1, 1958. At its birth, NASA was far behind the Soviet space program. The nation could only look to the sky anxiously and hope that it would be able to catch up.

In 1959, determined to put an American into orbit as soon as possible, NASA began recruiting its first group of space pilots, or astronauts, as NASA called them. The term "astronaut" is derived from two Greek words that mean "star sailor."

The first group of astronauts was drawn from the United States military. NASA asked each branch of the military to list all of its members who met certain specific qualifications. They had to be jet pilots with at least 1,500 hours of flying time under their belts. They had to have a college degree or the equivalent in practical experience. They had to be under the age of forty. Finally, they could not be any taller than 5 feet 11 inches tall (1.8 m). There was not enough room in the one-person Mercury capsule for anyone taller than that.

The Mercury 7

Five hundred pilots from each of the four branches of the United States military volunteered for the space program. After an exhausting round of physical and psychological tests, NASA chose just seven men to become the first astronauts—the so-called Mercury 7. Mercury was the name of NASA's first manned space program, designed to put a man into orbit around Earth and return him home safely. On May 5, 1961, NASA scored its first great success by sending Alan Shepard up high into Earth's atmosphere during a brief suborbital flight. He was the first American ever to travel to space. Less than a year

American astronauts pose with a model of the rocket that will carry Gemini spacecraft into space. Front row, right to left, are James Lovell, John Glenn, James McDivitt, Wally Schirra, and John Young. Second row, right to left, are Thomas Stafford, Neil Armstrong, Edward White, and Frank Borman. Standing on ladders are, from right, Charles Conrad and Elliot See.

later, on February 20, 1962, John Glenn became the first American to orbit Earth. Though still running behind the Soviets, NASA was catching up and gaining momentum.

In order to seize on NASA's early success and gain even more momentum, President John F. Kennedy made a very important speech to his country three weeks after Shepard's historic spaceflight. In it, he warned of the dangers of allowing the Soviet Union to gain control of space. In order to help win the global battle "now going on around the world between freedom and tyranny," Kennedy challenged the nation to commit itself to taking a leading role in space achievement, which he felt may be the key to the future of humankind. The first step toward this lofty goal would be both very specific and utterly fantastical, and on a very tight schedule. Kennedy proposed nothing less than, by the close of the 1960s, putting a man on the Moon and returning him safely to Earth.

At the time President Kennedy gave this historic and inspiring speech, NASA was already looking beyond Mercury toward its next manned space program—Gemini. The Gemini program was

On May 6, 1961, one day after returning from space, Alan Shepard traveled to Washington, D.C. In a ceremony at the White House, he received NASA's Distinguished Service Medal from President John F. Kennedy. Vice President Lyndon B. Johnson is standing second from right. A few days later, a parade in Shepard's honor was held in the nation's capital.

designed to serve as a bridge between the ground-breaking solo flights of Mercury and the upcoming manned lunar landings of the Apollo program. The Gemini spaceflights would develop and test the equipment, technology, and procedures that the Apollo missions would employ to fly a spacecraft to the Moon and land an astronaut on its surface. Because the program's spacecraft would be two-man

vehicles (rather than Mercury's one-man capsules), NASA named it Gemini after the constellation that is often represented visually by the twins Castor and Pollux.

In order to fill the astronaut slots made available by the new Gemini program, NASA again sent out invitations to military test pilots in September 1962. Two hundred fifty-three pilots were interviewed by NASA and given written exams to test their engineering and scientific knowledge. Nine men made the final cut and became astronaut trainees. One of them was James Lovell.

CHAPTER 2

LOVELL'S FIRST TRIP TO SPACE

After being accepted into NASA, James Lovell embarked upon a three-year course of intensive training and study. The physical training was exhausting. Astronaut trainees were subjected to a series of grueling ordeals designed to prepare them for the stresses of space travel. They rode a centrifuge—a capsule attached to a rapidly spinning mechanical arm—that simulated the crushing weight of gravitational forces (G forces) that an astronaut would feel during liftoff and reentry. When the centrifuge began spinning very rapidly and the G forces increased, trainees

could become dizzy and disoriented. Sometimes they even blacked out.

In order to simulate weightlessness, Lovell and the other Gemini astronauts were taken up in the "vomit comet"—a modified KC-135 transport plane. The plane, outfitted with a padded cabin, was put through a series of thirty or more steep ascents and controlled dives. This roller coaster–like motion resulted in brief periods of weightlessness as the plane crested and began nosing down into a dive. It also frequently resulted in prolonged bouts of nausea. Weightlessness training also involved long hours spent in buoyancy tanks—large tubs filled with water. Wearing scuba gear or space suits, the trainees would practice the sort of physical tasks they would need to accomplish in the difficult and often clumsy conditions of zero gravity.

Like the Mercury spacecraft, Gemini capsules were all scheduled to land in the ocean. The astronauts and capsule would then be retrieved, or picked up by military helicopters and brought to a nearby aircraft carrier. In case of an emergency or accidental landing on land, however, the astronaut trainees had to be prepared for survival in a wide range of harsh

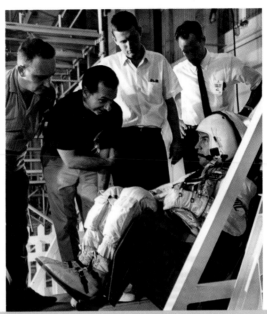

James Lovell undergoes weight and balance tests in preparation for an upcoming Gemini space-flight. He is surrounded by NASA technicians and representatives of the companies that designed and built the Gemini craft.

environments. For practice, trainees were dropped into jungles, deserts, and other extreme locales with a limited food and water supply. They were forced to develop the skills necessary to fend for themselves, hunt animals with basic tools, and tell the difference between safe and poisonous plants and snakes.

In addition to these physical challenges, Lovell and his fellow astronaut trainees were also put

through a demanding course of study. They spent much of the day in classes and lectures, learning all about emergency procedures and capsule hardware and operations. They also received a lot of valuable practice on a variety of flight simulators.

Lovell's First Assignment

As Lovell busied himself with training, preparations, and planning for the Gemini spaceflights, he received his first mission assignment. He would serve on the backup crew for *Gemini 4* (the first two Gemini flights were unmanned missions that were designed to test the safety and performance of the two-man spacecraft). The first manned Gemini spaceflight was *Gemini 3*, and it went off without a hitch. Virgil "Gus" Grissom and John Young were launched on March 25, 1965. The two men circled Earth three times before splashing down. During the flight, Grissom set a new record for being the first astronaut to visit space twice. He was one of NASA's original Mercury 7 astronauts and had first visited space in 1961 in *Mercury 4*.

The prime and backup crews of the *Gemini 4* spaceflight stand in their pressure suits behind a model of the Gemini spacecraft. From left to right are Edward White, James McDivitt, Frank Borman, and James Lovell. White and McDivitt were the main crew, and Borman and Lovell were the backup.

As a backup pilot for *Gemini 4*, Lovell had to prepare carefully and thoroughly for the spaceflight, as if he were indeed being sent to space. In the event that the primary crew—James A. McDivitt and Edward H. White—could not fly due to illness, injury, or accident, Lovell would have to be prepared to step in at a moment's notice and perform all the necessary tasks and procedures associated with the mission.

As it turned out, McDivitt and White made it to launch day in good health and with no mishaps and were cleared for takeoff. On June 3, 1965, they soared beyond Earth's atmosphere and into space. This was the Gemini program's second manned spaceflight and its first long-duration mission (it would last more than four days).

Gemini 4 was a great success, proving that man and machine could safely remain in space for prolonged periods with no ill effects. The Gemini program was now ready to move forward and attempt more ambitious missions that would more closely simulate the eventual Moon shots of Apollo. This meant that it would soon be James Lovell's turn to go into space. His days of watching and waiting were almost over. He had been assigned to pilot *Gemini* 7.

Gemini 6 and 7

Gemini 6 and 7 were to be simultaneous missions designed mainly to test rendezvous techniques between two manned spacecraft. If successful, these would be the techniques used during Apollo

The prime and backup crews of the *Gemini 7* spaceflight pose alongside a model of the Gemini spacecraft. Kneeling, from left to right, are Michael Collins and James Lovell. Standing, from left to right, are Edward White and Frank Borman. Lovell and Borman formed the mission's main crew, while White and Collins served as backup.

missions when the lunar module—fresh from its visit to the Moon—would have to rendezvous and dock with the orbiting command module. Once docked, the astronauts who had landed on the Moon would be reunited with the astronaut left behind in the command module, and the crew and craft would then begin the journey back to Earth.

James Lovell *(seated, left)* and Frank Borman *(seated, right)* review mission requirements for the *Gemini 7* spaceflight. Leaning in at left is Michael Collins, the mission's backup pilot. *Gemini 7* would be the longest spaceflight in history up to that point and would be the first major test of rendezvous techniques .

It was finally time for James Lovell to take his first trip to space. He and his fellow crew member, Frank Borman, would be in orbit for just under fourteen days, by far the longest spaceflight in history up to that point. Once again, NASA was mainly interested in observing how well the crew and craft would hold up during such a long time spent in zero gravity. The mission's

James Lovell walks to the launch pad elevator that will carry him up to the *Gemini 7* spacecraft perched on top on a Titan II rocket on December 4, 1965.

other major objective was to provide a rendezvous target for *Gemini 6*, which would be orbiting Earth at the same time as Lovell and Borman. The crew members of *Gemini 6*—Walter "Wally" Schirra and Thomas Stafford—would use manual and automatic controls to maneuver close to the *Gemini 7* capsule, simulating the docking procedures that would be required during a Moon shot. In addition, for the first time in NASA history, the *Gemini 7* astronauts

The Titan II rocket carrying the *Gemini 7* spacecraft is launched from Cape Canaveral, Florida, on December 4, 1965, at 2:30 PM. On board are James Lovell and Frank Borman, who will remain in orbit around Earth for just under two weeks.

would attempt to move around and work in a so-called shirtsleeve environment. Once in orbit, they would remove their bulky space suits and move about in a more lightweight pressure suit.

The plan was for *Gemini 6* to be launched first and for *Gemini 7* to follow it up into space. A minor technical problem delayed the launch of *Gemini 6*, however, so Lovell and Borman were sent into space first, on December 4, 1965. *Gemini 6*, now renamed *Gemini 6-A*, was finally launched on December 15. For the first time ever, two American spacecraft were orbiting Earth at the same time.

Stationkeeping

While waiting for *Gemini 6-A* to launch and draw near them, Lovell and Borman spent the first five days of their mission conducting experiments and spacecraft tests. One of these tests involved a procedure called stationkeeping.

Stationkeeping refers to the way spacecraft circle, approach, and back away from each other. During the lunar missions of Apollo, the lunar

module would be carried into space within the Apollo craft's second-stage rocket (a rocket that fires after the main rocket has run out of fuel and separated from the craft). Once the second-stage rocket was spent, the command module would separate from it, turn 180 degrees, maneuver back to the lunar module within the rocket, and dock with it. Then the docked modules would pull away from the rocket and travel on to the Moon.

Lovell and Borman tested the first part of this procedure soon after reaching Earth's orbit. Immediately after their spacecraft separated from its second-stage rocket, the astronauts began station-keeping exercises, repeatedly drawing to within 20 feet (6 m) of the rocket and pulling back to a distance of 50 miles (81 km) in a seventeen-minute period. Actual docking exercises would not occur till later Gemini missions.

A little more than five hours after *Gemini 6-A* was launched, it met up with *Gemini 7*, which was waiting in a prearranged location. The two space-crafts were supposed to draw as close together as they could, without actually touching. At one point, they approached within just 1 foot (30 centimeters) of each other, and the crews could see each other clearly through their capsule windows. The two spacecraft orbited nose to nose at about 17,500 miles per hour (28,164 kilometers per hour). They approached and withdrew from each

This is an artist's drawing that depicts the planned rendezvous of the *Gemini 6-A* and *7* spacecraft high above Earth. The exercise would be performed perfectly on December 15, 1965, with James Lovell and Frank Borman guiding *Gemini 7* to within 1 foot (30 cm) of *Gemini 6-A*, piloted by Wally Schirra and Thomas Stafford.

HIGH-ALTITUDE COMEDY

During the stationkeeping exercise between *Gemini 6-A* and *Gemini 7*—designed to simulate the docking between a command module and a lunar module after the lunar module's return from the Moon—the crews repeatedly radioed back and forth to each other, often cracking jokes in the process. When *Gemini 6-A* first arrived, Lovell radioed to them and said, "Hello there. What kept you?" When the two spacecraft passed over Hawaii together, Schirra made the comment, "There seems to be a lot of traffic up here." Borman replied to Schirra, "Call a policeman." At one point, Lovell radioed to Schirra that he thought he could see him moving his lips. Schirra radioed back to Lovell that his lips were moving because he was chewing gum!

other for almost five and a half hours, through three and a half orbits. This was the first time in history that two spacecraft were maneuvered by their crews into a rendezvous position. Previously, manned vehicles had rendezvoused with unmanned, passive craft.

Coming Home

Following the stationkeeping exercises, *Gemini 6-A* fired its thrusters and moved 30 miles (48 km) away from Lovell and Borman, as both craft entered a drifting "sleep period." The next day, December 16, *Gemini 6-A* headed for home. After only one full day in space, Schirra and Stafford splashed down 630 miles (1,014 km) southwest of Bermuda.

By the time *Gemini 6-A* returned to Earth, *Gemini 7* had already been in orbit for nearly two weeks. The rendezvous with *Gemini 6-A* had been important, but it was not Lovell and Borman's only job. During their mission, the two men had completed more than twenty important scientific experiments, including weather and

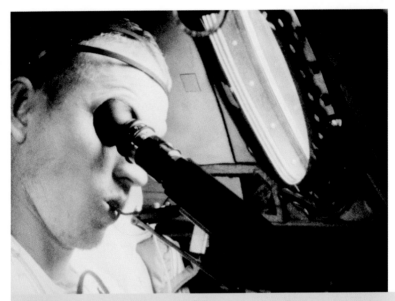

Frank Borman gazes through the inflight vision tester on *Gemini 7*. This machine was part of a series of vision experiments designed to measure astronauts' eyesight before, during, and after long duration spaceflights. NASA researchers hoped to learn how long-term exposure to zero gravity conditions affected eyesight.

terrain photography. Another experiment was called the in-flight sleep analysis investigation. During this experiment, Lovell had to wear electrodes attached to his head to record his brain activity and measure how much sleep he got during the long mission. The results would help determine whether a lack of sleep hurt his performance as a pilot. The knowledge gained by the experiment would then be used to teach other astronauts how to sleep better and longer while in space. Other experiments performed on *Gemini 7* collected data on such things as the crew's blood pressures, heart rates, body temperatures, and respiration (breathing). The information gathered would help identify the long-term effects on the human body of an extended stay in zero gravity.

Finally, on December 18, it was time for Lovell and Borman to head back to Earth. They had been in space for more than thirteen days and eighteen hours, orbiting Earth 206 times. NASA astronauts had again set a new record for the longest amount of time spent in space (a record that would not be broken again for another eight years). Lovell and Borman splashed down in the Pacific Ocean very close to the location of *Gemini 6-A*'s splashdown of two days earlier.

NASA was very pleased with the results of the *Gemini 6-A* and *Gemini 7* missions. The flights had proved that two NASA spacecraft could rendezvous in space, orbit side by side, and approach close enough to be able to dock. This success lay the groundwork for many future Gemini and Apollo spaceflights that would feature rendezvous

The *Gemini 7* spacecraft splashed down in the Pacific Ocean on December 18, 1965. James Lovell can be seen getting pulled out of the ocean and up to a navy rescue helicopter. Below him, Frank Borman sits in an inflatable raft next to the Gemini capsule.

and docking maneuvers. All in all, NASA felt that 1965 had been the American space program's most successful year so far.

In tribute to their achievement, the air force promoted Borman to colonel (from captain), while the navy promoted Lovell to captain (from lieutenant commander). The two men continued to travel together, though at a lower altitude. They took trips to several foreign countries, serving as goodwill ambassadors and providing good publicity for the American space program. The space race was tilting in the United States's favor, and NASA wanted the whole world to take notice.

Rather than taking a well-deserved vacation following his return from his overseas goodwill tour, Lovell immediately resumed flight training and preparation for his next spaceflight—*Gemini 12,* the final mission of the Gemini program.

CHAPTER 3

GEMINI 12

Gemini missions 8 through 11 were focused primarily on docking procedures and space walks. With the exception of *Gemini 9* (for which James Lovell served on the backup crew and whose docking exercises were canceled due to rocket malfunctions), each spaceflight was a great success. NASA was edging ever closer to putting a man on the Moon, though time was running out. President Kennedy's deadline of the end of the 1960s was fast approaching, and the Apollo program had not yet begun its lunar missions.

James Lovell and his *Gemini 12* crewmate, Edwin "Buzz" Aldrin, were launched on November 11, 1966. It was Veterans' Day in the United States, and this was the first NASA space launch to take place on a national holiday. The mission had several objectives, including a docking with a Gemini Agena Target Vehicle (GATV)—an unmanned spacecraft used for docking practice—launched ninety minutes before *Gemini 12*, three space walks, and a reentry controlled by computer rather than manual guidance controls.

Less than four hours after launch, *Gemini 12* rendezvoused with the GATV. After twenty-eight minutes of careful maneuvering, Lovell and Aldrin were able to dock with the other spacecraft. The onboard radar was malfunctioning, so much of the rendezvous and docking was done the old-fashioned way—by calculating distances and spacecraft positions using mathematical formulas and simply looking out the window to "eyeball" the situation.

The next step of the test was to see if, once docked, *Gemini 12* could use the GATV's propulsion system to lift the combined craft to a higher orbit. Technical problems with the GATV resulted in the cancellation of this exercise, however. NASA

This photograph, taken from the *Gemini 12* spacecraft, shows the Agena Target Vehicle floating in space during a successful tether experiment. Beneath the target vehicle can be seen parts of Mexico, Arizona, and New Mexico, including the Tucson, Phoenix, and Painted Desert areas.

ground controllers had noticed that the GATV was losing pressure in its thrust chamber. They thought that, under these circumstances, trying to use the GATV to carry *Gemini 12* into a higher orbit might pose a danger to the astronauts. Instead, Lovell and Aldrin moved into position to be able to witness a total eclipse over South America, which they photographed through the capsule windows.

Walking in Space

The first extra-vehicular activity (EVA; a space walk) of the mission took place the next morning, November 12. *Gemini 12* was still docked with the GATV. Aldrin, in his full space suit, stood on a seat below the spacecraft's hatch, opened the hatch door above him, and stuck his upper body out into open space. During the two hours and twenty-nine minutes in which he stood halfway out of the space-craft, he accomplished several tasks. Aldrin mounted a special camera to the side of the spacecraft that would be used in a later space walk. He also installed a handrail that would help him reach the GATV during a space walk on the following day. Finally, Aldrin conducted an experiment involving the collection of extremely tiny meteorites.

Aldrin's second EVA occurred on the morning of November 13. Aldrin exited the capsule but remained attached to it by a 30-foot (9-m) tether (a long cord). While he was outside the spacecraft, Aldrin again performed several basic manual tasks. During one of the more difficult tasks, he moved from the Gemini capsule to the GATV with the help of the handrail he had installed the day before.

Once he reached the GATV, he removed a 98-foot (30-m) tether stored inside the target vehicle and attached it to the Gemini capsule for a later experiment. Periodically taking two-minute rests to avoid exhaustion, Aldrin returned to the capsule after more than two hours of work in open space. At one point during the EVA, Aldrin must have knocked up against the Gemini capsule without knowing it. Lovell radioed to him, "Hey, easy, easy, you're shaking up the whole spacecraft."

Two and a half hours after Aldrin completed his space walk, he and Lovell were ready to begin the tether experiment. They programmed the GATV to turn the two spacecraft, still docked to each other, so that they were vertical, pointing down toward Earth. Then, they undocked the Gemini spacecraft from the target vehicle and moved away from it. Though undocked, the two vehicles were still attached by the tether Aldrin had attached. They moved the Gemini craft away from the GATV so they could extend the tether until it was pulled tight. Once the two vehicles were attached only by the tether, it was hard for Lovell to keep his spacecraft straight. It tended to

During the *Gemini 12* spaceflight, Buzz Aldrin performed three EVAs. This November 13, 1966, photograph shows his second EVA, during which he fully exited the spacecraft and moved around outside while attached to a 30-foot (9-m) tether. In total, Aldrin spent five and a half hours outside the *Gemini 12* spacecraft.

roll and tumble, but he eventually learned how to keep the craft steady.

Gemini 12 continued to orbit Earth while attached to the GATV. This experiment was very important to NASA because it proved that a spacecraft could orbit Earth by "borrowing" power from a rocket. By using a rocket's power instead of its own, a spacecraft could save its own fuel. After the two vehicles had been joined by the tether for more

TAKING OUT THE TRASH

With the successful completion of the GATV tether experiment, *Gemini 12* was nearing the end of its mission. Aldrin had one more space walk to perform, however, before he and Lovell could return home. During this EVA, Aldrin did not actually leave the spacecraft. He stood upon his seat again, with the upper half of his body outside the craft. He took more terrain, astronomical, and weather photographs, and conducted some more scientific experiments. A lot of equipment they no longer needed was also jettisoned (thrown overboard). Getting rid of unnecessary heavy equipment would lighten the ship for the return home, save fuel, and make reentry easier. After Aldrin had thrown several pieces of equipment—and even some trash—into space, Lovell commented that *Gemini 12* was the litter-bug spaceflight. The trash and equipment dropped out of the spacecraft is still orbiting somewhere high above Earth today!

than four hours, Lovell released the tether and *Gemini 12* was flying on its own again.

Gemini Reaches the End

On this flight, reentry would be controlled automatically, and the new system worked beautifully. Lovell and Aldrin splashed down in the Atlantic Ocean at 2:21 PM on November 15, less than 3 miles (5 km) away from their target site. Millions of people watching television heard mission control say to the two astronauts, "Smile, you're on the tube." The two men felt very proud and happy that their mission was successful. Aldrin had set a record for the longest total amount of EVAs during one mission—five hours and thirty-two minutes. Lovell had also set a new and important record. He became the world record holder for the most amount of time spent in space. During *Gemini 7* and *Gemini 12*, Lovell had been in space for a total of 425 hours and nine minutes.

The end of the *Gemini 12* mission was also the end of the entire Gemini program. NASA was extremely pleased and felt that all of Gemini's

Following splashdown of the *Gemini 12* spacecraft in the Atlantic Ocean on November 15, 1966, James Lovell and Buzz Aldrin were taken by a navy rescue helicopter to the aircraft carrier USS *Wasp*. In this photograph, Lovell *(left)* and Aldrin receive an official welcome from the carrier's captain.

goals had been met. Twelve Gemini missions had been launched, ten of them manned. Each mission ended with the astronauts returning safely back to Earth. NASA could now move forward into the Apollo program—the program that would one day take Americans to the Moon.

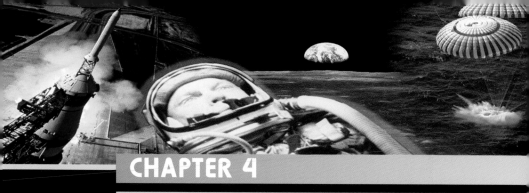

CHAPTER 4

APOLLO 8 AND THE GIANT LEAP

The Gemini program had been conceived as a testing ground for the equipment and procedures that would be used in the Moon shots of the later Apollo program. Since the Gemini program had been successfully completed, it was now time for the Apollo missions to achieve the late John F. Kennedy's goal of putting an American on the Moon. Kennedy, who had been assassinated in 1963, had set a deadline for the first Moon landing—the end of the 1960s. It was now 1966, and time was getting short.

Like Gemini before it, the Apollo program started out with unmanned flights. In 1966, the year Gemini was completed, three unmanned Apollo flights lifted off from Launch Pad 39-A at Cape Kennedy (the former Cape Canaveral, renamed in honor of the president, following his assassination). All future Apollo flights would be launched from this pad. At the same time, a new NASA flight center was built in Houston, Texas. From this point on, spaceflights would all be controlled from this center. It was called the NASA Manned Spaceflight Center, but it became known all around the world simply as mission control.

A Tragic Setback for Apollo

By the beginning of 1967, everything was going well at NASA. It seemed that the United States would indeed be able to reach its goal of sending a man to the Moon by decade's end. So far, there had been no major problems with any of their Mercury or Gemini spaceflights. NASA's technology, know-how, and astronaut corps seemed more than up to the task. Meanwhile, the Soviet Union's space program was

The *Apollo 1* crew is seen here in their space suits less than two months before a capsule fire that broke out during spacecraft testing took their lives on January 27, 1967. From left to right are Gus Grissom, Edward White, and Roger Chaffee. The inset shows the outside of the *Apollo 1* capsule. The damage to the metal shows how intense the heat generated by the fire was.

making its own advances, though it was lagging somewhat behind NASA.

Just as NASA's momentum toward the Moon began to build, however, tragedy struck the United States space program. The three astronauts who had been chosen for the first manned Apollo mission—Gus Grissom, Roger Chaffee, and Edward White—were killed in a fire while performing a systems test of their spacecraft.

This tragic accident shook the NASA family and saddened the entire nation. NASA was forced to put the Apollo program on hold for more than a year while engineers and investigators tried to figure out what had gone wrong. Stricken by the loss of three of the space program's best astronauts, NASA made the necessary changes to improve the safety of future Apollo capsules and tried to get back on track again.

Despite the tragic loss of Grissom, Chaffee, and White, NASA's focus never wavered. Following the release of the accident investigation report and the completion of the necessary capsule redesigns, the Apollo program was restarted. Astronauts and engineers alike were still determined to reach the

Moon by decade's end, inspired now not only by President Kennedy's words but also by the sacrifice of Apollo's first three astronauts.

The First Apollo Spaceflights

The Apollo program was designed as a step-by-step process. The first step would consist of unmanned tests of the launch rockets and spacecraft. The second group of missions would be manned tests of the command service module (CSM)—the primary spaceship—in orbit around Earth. The lunar module (LM)—the smaller craft that would detach from the CSM and land on the Moon—was to be added for the following series of missions. A dress rehearsal mission that would reach and orbit the Moon but not land on it was next. Finally, several actual lunar landings would occur toward the end of the Apollo program.

On November 9, 1967, *Apollo 4* was launched. It was the first spaceflight of the program to bear the Apollo title, though Grissom, White, and Chaffee's flight was renamed *Apollo 1* in tribute to the lost astronauts. *Apollo 4* was an unmanned suborbital test

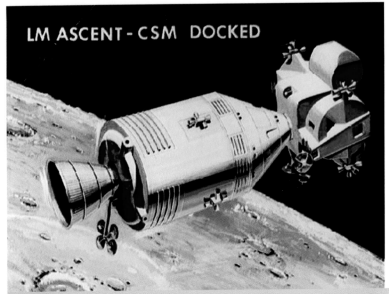

LM ASCENT - CSM DOCKED

This is an artist's drawing depicting an Apollo command service module (CSM) docked to a lunar module (LM). The combined Apollo spacecraft is shown orbiting above the lunar surface. Two of the three astronauts on an Apollo Moon landing mission would climb into the LM, which would then separate from the CSM and travel down to the Moon's surface.

of the Saturn V rocket that would carry future Apollo capsules into space. *Apollo 5*, also unmanned, followed in January 1968 and featured the first test of the lunar module, which was sent into orbit around Earth.

Two and a half months later, *Apollo 6*—the final unmanned Apollo test flight—was launched and provided a test of the new command service module. The Apollo command module (CM) was a cone-shaped craft that served as a command and communications center. Attached to it was the cylinder-shaped service module (SM), which provided the crew's life-support elements (such as oxygen and water) and the main propulsion (thrusting) and maneuvering (steering) capability. When attached, the combined modules were called the command service module (CSM). The service module would be jettisoned just before reentry. The command module would then fall back down through Earth's atmosphere and splash down in the ocean, where it would bob and float until a helicopter came to retrieve the astronauts and capsule.

Finally, in October 1968, NASA was ready to launch the first manned Apollo mission—*Apollo 7*—and the first manned mission since the *Apollo 1* tragedy. The astronauts chosen for the spaceflight were Wally Schirra, Donn Eisele, and Walter Cunningham. Their mission was simply to take the CSM up into Earth's orbit and make sure the rockets, CSM, crew, and mission control were all working—individually and together—as designed. *Apollo 7* launched on October 11, orbited Earth 163 times, and splashed down in the Atlantic

Ocean on October 22. The mission went well, the astronauts were safe, and *Apollo 7* was declared a success. A full dress rehearsal for a Moon landing was next, and James Lovell would be chosen for this historic and important trial run.

Apollo 8

Apollo 8 was to be a very important mission for many reasons. It would be the first manned test of the CSM in a cislunar flight (traveling between Earth and the Moon) as well as in lunar orbit. It would also be the first important test of a crew's performance during the journey to the Moon and once inserted into lunar orbit. The quality of communications between the CSM and mission control from the great distance separating the Moon and Earth would be an area of particular interest. Finally, *Apollo 8* would represent the first time that any human being had seen the far side of the Moon with his own eyes. In September and November 1968, two Soviet unmanned craft had made the journey, and NASA wanted to do them one better, fearing a Soviet manned lunar mission was near. The

The three astronauts of *Apollo 8* prepare for centrifuge training in January 1968. From left to right are William Anders, lunar module pilot; James Lovell, command module pilot; and Frank Borman, commander. The inset shows the logo for the *Apollo 8* mission, which would be the first manned spaceflight in history to enter lunar orbit.

Apollo 8 astronauts would take high-resolution photographs of proposed landing sites on the lunar surface for future Apollo Moon landings, in addition to other locations of scientific interest.

James Lovell was thrilled to be one of the three men chosen for this historic first mission to the Moon. He would serve as command module pilot. His crewmates were William A. Anders, lunar module pilot, and Frank Borman, mission commander. Lovell and Borman had flown into space together two years earlier, aboard *Gemini 7*. Together, they had set a new record for the longest time spent in space, almost fourteen days. *Apollo 8* would be an even more dramatic and groundbreaking flight for Lovell and Borman, however. This time, they would orbit the Moon, not just Earth. They would be the first humans to travel beyond Earth's orbit. No human being before them had ever traveled so far, so fast, or drew so close to another celestial body.

Apollo 8 launched on December 21, 1968. After only eleven minutes, *Apollo 8* was in Earth's orbit. During its second orbit, the third stage of the Saturn V rocket fired, hurling the Apollo spacecraft toward the Moon at 25,000 miles per hour (40,234 km/h).

Soon, *Apollo 8* was sending the first television pictures of Earth back to mission control for the whole world to see. The images were not very clear at all, and some viewers were disappointed. The Earth looked like a big fuzzy white spot. On the next day, however, after the spacecraft had left Earth's atmosphere, the pictures sent to Earth from *Apollo 8* were much sharper and clearer. The world could finally see their planet as Lovell and the other two astronauts were seeing it—as a colorful globe shining brilliantly in rich shades of blue, bright white, brown, and green, surrounded by the velvety blackness of space. We may be used to such photographs today, but no one on Earth had ever seen anything like it in 1968.

The Far Side of the Moon

It took *Apollo 8* more than two days to reach the Moon. Early on December 24, Christmas Eve, the spacecraft entered the Moon's gravitational field. The Moon's gravity pulled *Apollo 8* into its orbit, and the craft began coasting behind it, out of sight of Earth. Once it disappeared behind the Moon, the spacecraft was out of contact with mission control because the radio signals were blocked. For more than thirty minutes, mission control could not be certain that all was well with the astronauts. While out of sight, Lovell fired the thrusters of the service module's propulsion system, and the spacecraft emerged from behind the Moon. Radio contact was reestablished, and everyone at mission control—and around the world—breathed a sigh of relief.

This is a photograph taken by the *Apollo 8* astronauts of Earth rising above the Moon's horizon.

While the astronauts were passing around the far side of the Moon, they took photos of the lunar surface. Orbiting from 69 to 195 miles (111 to 314 km) above the lunar surface, the men mapped out what they saw below them. They tried to find the best sites for a future Moon landing, stretches of terrain that were relatively smooth and flat. Every afternoon, the astronauts transmitted down to Earth a live television broadcast, including images of the lunar surface, and described exactly what they were seeing.

Anders reported that the lunar surface must have been hit with lots of meteorites because the Moon was covered with holes and craters. Lovell located the area known as the Sea of Tranquility. He said that it looked like a dirty, gray beach. Borman said that the surface looked like a "vast, huge, harsh, and lonely place." He said he did not think it would be a very nice place to live and work.

Despite the harsh beauty of the lunar surface, the astronauts were mesmerized. As Lovell said in a 1994 documentary of the Apollo program, *Moon Shot,* "We were like three schoolkids looking into a candy store window—our noses were pressed against the window, and we looked at those ancient craters as they slid on by, and we forgot the flight plan for a while and forgot really how dangerous this all was because it was really something unique."

A Safe Return

The next day, early Christmas morning, *Apollo 8* again disappeared behind the Moon. This would be its last orbit before returning home. Once more out of contact with mission control, Lovell fired the service module thrusters.

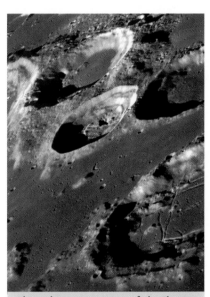

This close-up view of the lunar surface was taken by the *Apollo 8* astronauts. The craters range in diameter from 20 to 45 miles (35 to 70 km).

If they did not fire properly, the spacecraft would not be able to propel itself out of lunar orbit back to Earth. It would remain in orbit around the Moon until gravity eventually caused it to crash onto the lunar surface. This lurking anxiety increased when *Apollo 8* did not emerge from behind the Moon at the correct time. They were six minutes late, and mission control was getting worried.

Happily, *Apollo 8* finally reemerged from behind the Moon. Lovell's voice was heard over the radio, and everyone at mission control cheered. Once radio contact was reestablished, it was learned that the thrusters had worked perfectly, propelling the spacecraft free of lunar orbit at about 5,500 miles per hour (8,851 km/h). On its way home, *Apollo 8* gained speed as Earth's gravitational pull began to pull the capsule toward the home planet. When the spacecraft reentered Earth's atmosphere, it was traveling at about 25,000 miles per hour (40,234 km/h). At this speed, the craft had to come in at just the right angle. If it came in at too steep an angle, it would burn up. If it came in at too shallow an angle, it would be bounced back into space again.

CHRISTMAS IN SPACE

The *Apollo 8* astronauts spent the Christmas holiday in space. On Christmas Eve, Borman said he was supposed to be at his church, leading a prayer. Instead, he said a prayer for worldwide peace and asked mission control to send it along to his church and to the whole world. The three men took turns reading the first ten verses of the book of Genesis, the first book of the Bible, which includes the Creation story. They then offered the entire world a heartfelt holiday greeting: "Good night, good luck, a Merry Christmas, and God bless all of you—all of you on the good Earth" (as quoted by the James Lovell page of the Encyclopedia Astronautica Web site). *TV Guide* later claimed that one out of every four persons on Earth— almost one billion people—heard this holiday greeting from space through either radio or television broadcasts.

After jettisoning the service module, the command module continued on its fiery path toward the Pacific Ocean. As the capsule began to be slowed by Earth's dense atmosphere, the astronauts began experiencing the force of six Gs—six times the force of gravity usually felt on Earth. When the capsule slowed to 300 miles per hour (483 km/h), three small parachutes opened, further slowing the capsule. When it was falling to Earth at about 140 miles per hour (225 km/h), the main parachutes opened. *Apollo 8* gently splashed down 1,100 miles (1,770 km) southwest of Hawaii, only 5,000 yards (4.6 km) from the aircraft carrier that was waiting to meet it.

Lovell, Borman, and Anders had orbited the Moon ten times in twenty hours—the first humans to do so—and they had gathered information that would be extremely valuable when it was time for NASA to finally land a man on the Moon's surface. For several months after their historic spaceflight, the astronauts and their families toured the country. Everywhere they went, the three astronauts of *Apollo 8* were viewed as heroes and pioneers. All three families were invited to attend the Super

Bowl in January. The astronauts led the crowd there in the Pledge of Allegiance. They received standing ovations. They gave speeches to huge crowds. They attended lots of parties and parades. They received hundreds of thousands of letters of congratulations from people all over the world.

Lovell, Borman, and Anders had proved that humans could be sent to the Moon, orbit around it, and hover less than 100 miles (161 km) above its surface. This achievement alone was a triumph that few would have believed possible only a generation earlier. The next big step, however, was to actually land an astronaut on the lunar surface. The remaining Apollo missions would work to achieve just that.

Man on the Moon

Apollo 9 would provide the first test of the lunar module, as the crew practiced docking with the CSM, undocking, flying the LM independently, and redocking with the CSM. The tests went beautifully. The lunar module's maiden voyage was a great success. *Apollo 10* was the final dress rehearsal before *Apollo 11* would finally make John F. Kennedy's dream come true by landing an American astronaut on the Moon. The mission followed the exact same procedures as *Apollo 11* without actually touching down upon the lunar surface. The American space program finally stood on the brink of landing on the Moon. One of the greatest adventures in American history was about to begin.

The three astronauts chosen for *Apollo 11* had all flown in space before. Neil Armstrong was the mission commander. He had been on *Gemini 8*, the first spacecraft to successfully complete a docking in space. Buzz Aldrin was the LM pilot. Aldrin had been with Lovell on *Gemini 12*, the final Gemini mission. He had gotten to walk in space several times during that mission. The CSM pilot was Michael Collins. As part of *Gemini 10*, Collins had been the first human to make contact with another vehicle in space. He had also practiced docking procedures on that mission, and that experience would be important during *Apollo 11*. Collins would be flying the CSM and would be responsible for redocking with the LM after Armstrong and Aldrin had visited the Moon. The crew nicknamed their CSM *Columbia*. Their LM was called the *Eagle*.

More than a billion people around the world watched on television as *Apollo 11* was launched on July 16, 1969. More than 2,000 journalists from more than fifty countries watched in person at the launch pad in Florida. Almost 250,000 miles (400,000 km) and more than three days later, *Apollo 11* reached the Moon.

This is the official emblem of the *Apollo 11* spaceflight, the first manned lunar landing in history.

The Giant Leap

Finally, on July 20, the thrilling day of the first Moon landing arrived. The lunar module, the *Eagle*, separated from the CSM and began its descent to the lunar surface. "The *Eagle* has wings," reported Armstrong to mission control. After Armstrong and Aldrin safely touched down on the lunar surface, Armstrong said, "The *Eagle* has landed," a phrase that soon became famous all over the world.

Buzz Aldrin stands next to the American flag he and Neil Armstrong have just set up on the lunar surface. He and Armstrong had just become the first people in history to set foot on the Moon. The lunar module can be seen to the right. The photograph was taken by Armstrong, who can be seen reflected in Aldrin's face mask.

Armstrong left the *Eagle* first. He stepped slowly down the 10-foot (3-m) ladder. On the way down, he turned on a TV camera so the millions of people watching television could see what he was seeing. When his left foot finally hit the surface of the Moon, he uttered yet another phrase that was destined to enter the history books: "That's one small step for man, one giant leap for mankind."

During the next two hours, Armstrong and Aldrin completed many tasks on the Moon, including the collection of soil and rock samples. Before returning to the *Eagle*, they marked the site of their landing with an American flag. There was also a plaque attached to the legs of the lunar module. The legs would remain behind after Armstrong and Aldrin blasted off in the *Eagle* from the lunar surface back to Collins and the CSM. The plaque reads, "Here men from the planet Earth first set foot upon the Moon July 1969, A.D. We came in peace for all mankind." The plaque was signed by the three *Apollo 11* astronauts and by the United States president at the time, Richard Nixon.

Blastoff from the lunar surface and the rendezvous with Collins and the CSM went flawlessly. The *Apollo 11* astronauts returned home on July 24, splashing down near Hawaii. President Kennedy had wanted the United States to land a man on the Moon by the end of the decade. NASA had accomplished that goal with only five months to spare. On the night that *Apollo 11* came home, someone left a bouquet of flowers on President Kennedy's grave at Arlington National Cemetery in Virginia. The flowers had a note attached. It read, "Mr. President, the *Eagle* has landed."

CHAPTER 5

THE RESCUE OF
APOLLO 13

The United States had achieved the lofty goal it had set for itself by successfully putting a man on the Moon and returning him safely to Earth. Despite this stunning triumph, however, the American space program was not interested in resting on its laurels. The Apollo program still had a lot of work ahead of it before it would be completed, including six more Moon landings. James Lovell would command one of these missions.

Lovell would have to wait eight months until his own lunar mission was launched. First came

Apollo 12, launched on November 14, 1969. Like *Apollo 11*, it was an almost flawless mission that landed two men on the Moon and brought them back safely. NASA and its astronauts were starting to make space travel look easy. Now it was James Lovell's turn.

Yet, Lovell's dream of landing on the Moon, for which he had worked so long and hard, would almost end in disaster. *Apollo 13* would not fulfill any of its mission goals but would prove that space-flight had by no means become routine, safe, and predictable. Space was still unconquered.

Bad Omens

One of the first men in history to reach the Moon, James Lovell would now get his chance to walk upon its surface. *Apollo 13* was the mission he had trained so hard for during his eight years with NASA. Lovell was assigned to be the mission's commander. Fred W. Haise Jr. was named the pilot of the lunar module, which was nicknamed *Aquarius*. John L. Swigert Jr. would serve as the pilot of the command service module, nicknamed

This is a portrait of the original prime crew for the *Apollo 13* spaceflight. From left to right are James Lovell, Ken Mattingly, and Fred Haise. Because Mattingly had been exposed to measles—which he had never had as a child or an adult—in the weeks leading up to the mission, he was not allowed to fly.

Odyssey. The term "odyssey" refers to a long, eventful journey full of changes in fortune. When the crew of *Apollo 13* chose this nickname, they had no idea how appropriate it would be.

Bad omens seemed to hover around *Apollo 13* from the beginning, starting with its "unlucky" mission number. The astronauts did not want to listen to the superstitious people who said that thirteen was an

GROUNDED BY MEASLES

As if the cascade of thirteens was not bad enough, one of *Apollo 13*'s original crew members had been removed due to German measles (an illness with thirteen letters in its name!). Ken Mattingly, who was slated to serve as CSM pilot, had been exposed to German measles by the backup LM pilot, Charlie Duke. NASA doctors determined that Mattingly had no immunity to the measles and was in danger of coming down with a case of them. He had to be removed from the roster and was replaced by John Swigert.

John Swigert

unlucky number. It did not bother them that their launch time was set for 2:13 PM Eastern Standard Time, which was 1:13 PM at mission control in Houston. They did not seem to mind that 1:13 PM was equivalent to 13:13 in military time (a twenty-four-hour timekeeping system that NASA also used).

There were many thirteens related to their mission, but the crew members felt far from unlucky. They were being given the opportunity to travel to the Moon and walk on its surface. They felt like the luckiest men alive.

Apollo 13, however, did turn out to be an almost catastrophically unlucky mission. Not only would the three men not land on the Moon, they would almost not make it back to their home on Earth.

A Rocky Start

The problems started only five and a half minutes after liftoff from the Kennedy Space Center on April 11, 1970. Lovell felt a small vibration that was not normal. One of the engines of the second-stage Saturn rocket had shut down two minutes earlier

A Saturn V rocket takes off on April 11, 1970, carrying *Apollo 13* and its crew into space. James Lovell, Fred Haise, and John Swigert were embarking on the greatest, most hair-raising adventure of their lives.

than scheduled. In order to be able to put *Apollo 13* into the proper orbit following this malfunction, the other four engines continued to burn half a minute longer than planned, and the third-stage Saturn rocket burned for an extra nine seconds. By the time *Apollo 13* entered Earth's orbit, the spacecraft was forty-four seconds behind schedule. That does not sound like a long time, but during spaceflights, every second and sometimes every fraction of a second counts. The flight plans and fuel use are so precisely calculated that even tiny delays can create a chain reaction of errors resulting in mission failure.

Once into orbit, however, things soon settled down, and the mission began to proceed as planned. The next major task was separation of the command service module from the Saturn rocket and rendezvous and docking with the lunar module. Swigert successfully separated the CSM from the rocket. He then turned the capsule around and moved in to dock with the LM housed in the rocket. Soon *Odyssey* and *Aquarius* were docked together, separated from the rocket, and headed toward the Moon. Lovell and his fellow crew members were on their way!

"Houston, We've Had a Problem"

Everything went very smoothly over the next two days while *Apollo 13* traveled the long distance to the Moon. According to NASA's Web page devoted to the *Apollo 13* mission, forty-six hours into the flight, Joe Kerwin, the mission's capsule communicator (capcom; the one person responsible for relaying messages and instructions between the astronauts and mission control), said, "The spacecraft is in real good shape as far as we are concerned.

We're bored to tears down here." Many at NASA felt this was the smoothest Apollo flight yet, despite the early glitches. This pleasant boredom was about to be shattered, however.

On April 13—yet another ill-omened thirteen—the crew filmed a live forty-nine–minute broadcast intended for American television (spaceflight had come to seem so routine for viewers, however, that the major networks decided not to run the broadcast). The crew offered viewers a tour of the CSM and LM and demonstrated what it was like to live and work in the weightless conditions of space. Nine minutes after Lovell wished America good night and signed off, something went terribly wrong.

The crew was getting ready for a rest period and performing some end-of-day housekeeping. Swigert had just received a request from mission control to turn the fans on in the spacecraft's oxygen tanks. The fans would help stir up the tanks, which were giving low-pressure readings. Several seconds after stirring the tanks, the *Apollo 13* crew heard a loud bang. The spacecraft began to vibrate. A yellow warning light began blinking on the instrument panel, indicating that the spacecraft was

NASA astronauts and flight controllers monitor their computers as they keep track of events on board *Apollo 13* from the mission operations control room of the mission control center, in Houston, Texas. Alan Shepard, the first American in space, is seated at far right.

losing electrical power. According to NASA's detailed timeline of the accident, Swigert radioed to mission control, "OK, Houston, we've had a problem here." Mission control asked him to repeat what he said. At this point, Lovell cut in, "Houston, we've had a problem."

When the fans were turned on, several short circuits occurred in fuel cell 3, which supplied

This is a photograph of the badly damaged service module of the *Apollo 13* spacecraft. It was taken from the window of the combined command and lunar modules after the service module was jettisoned in preparation for reentry into Earth's atmosphere.

power to the oxygen tank fans. The short circuits ignited some wire insulation and fire spread along the wires to the side of oxygen tank 2. This caused the temperature and pressure to increase in the oxygen tank. The sudden change in pressure caused the spacecraft to vibrate. Tank 2 then exploded, causing a tank line or valve in oxygen tank 1 to burst. As oxygen began to build up in bay 4 of the service module, the bay's cover was blown off, striking an antenna and causing some of the craft's fuel cells and oxygen valves to shut down.

Mission control tried to fix the problem as more and more warning lights lit up on the instrument panel. Two of the spacecraft's three fuel cells—*Apollo 13*'s main source of electricity—were dead. Lovell realized immediately that this meant they would not be able to land on the Moon. They could not complete a lunar landing mission with only one fuel cell. Lovell was extremely disappointed, but he began to realize that more was at stake here than a canceled Moon landing.

Stranded in a Lifeboat

Not only had the *Apollo 13* spacecraft lost fuel, it was also losing oxygen at an alarming rate. One oxygen tank seemed to be completely empty, and the second was leaking oxygen rapidly. When Lovell looked out the CSM's window, he saw something streaming out into space. It was oxygen pouring out of the second oxygen tank. If the tank lost all its

oxygen, the final fuel cell would die, too, as would the astronauts. Less than half an hour after their cheerful television broadcast, Lovell and his crew members were suddenly facing the most dangerous of circumstances and the very real likelihood of death in space, 200,000 miles (321,869 km) away from home.

The CSM no longer had enough power to be able to simply turn around and race for home before the crew's oxygen and water supplies ran out. Instead, in order to conserve the CSM's precious and dwindling supply of fuel, oxygen, and water, Lovell, Haise, and Swigert would have to shut down the CSM and climb into the lunar module. Instead of taking them to the Moon, *Aquarius* would instead serve as a lifeboat, providing them with electricity, oxygen, and fuel until they could maneuver the spacecraft back into Earth's atmosphere.

With only fifteen minutes of power left in the command service module, Lovell, Swigert, and Haise entered the lunar module. The LM was designed for less than fifty hours of use by two astronauts, but the three *Apollo 13* crew members would need it powered up for almost twice that much time in order to get back to Earth quickly. Time was critical. The

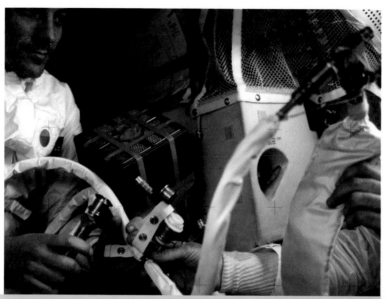

The crew of *Apollo 13* had to deal with a sudden buildup of poisonous carbon dioxide in the lunar module. The astronauts were forced to build a home-made air filter made out of materials they had available to them up in space, such as water bags, hoses, tape, and socks.

spacecraft had to return home as soon as possible because both power and water were in extremely short supply. Before the explosion, *Apollo 13* had been placed on a lunar landing course. Scarce fuel now had to be used to shift the spacecraft back onto a course to Earth that would take it around the far side of the Moon. The plan was to use the LM's propulsion system to periodically fire its thrusters,

speeding the spacecraft to the Moon, around it, and then back to Earth. The firing of the thrusters would help speed the spacecraft's return home, as would the trip around the Moon. The Moon's gravitational pull would serve as a slingshot, hurling *Apollo 13* around its far side back toward Earth.

Lovell, Swigert, and Haise had to hope that the LM would keep them safe for the remainder of the trip. They also had to hope that the CSM, when powered back up, would have enough remaining power to propel them out of Earth's orbit, down into Earth's atmosphere, and toward a safe splashdown back home.

Fighting for Survival

Trying to conserve power and water, Lovell and his crewmates shut down all nonessential systems in the LM, reducing energy use to a fifth of normal. With much of the electricity turned off, the spacecraft's heating system was shut down. Temperatures in the CSM plummeted to 38° Fahrenheit (3.3° Celsius), and the walls and sensitive instruments became slick with moisture. It was a little warmer in the LM but still very uncomfortable. NASA estimated that the crew would run out of water five hours before re-entry. It was not only the astronauts who needed the water; to prevent overheating, the spacecraft itself needed to be cooled by water. Since the craft needed it more than they did, the *Apollo 13* crew drank only 6 ounces (.18 liters) a day over four days, a fifth of their normal intake. They all became dehydrated, despite relying on fruit juices to replace their water supply. Lovell would lose 14 pounds (6.4 kilograms) during this mission. The entire crew lost more than 30 pounds (13.6 kg) total.

The crew took turns crawling into the dark CSM and trying to get some rest on their sleep couches. The cold kept them awake, however. They did not even have enough energy to dig out two blankets that were buried under heavy equipment. Lovell told mission control that they felt as cold as frogs in a frozen pond! NASA began to worry that the fatigue, physical stress, and sleep loss would begin to affect the astronauts' judgment and ability to function.

As if all this were not enough, carbon dioxide, a potentially deadly gas contained in every breath we exhale, started to build up in the lunar module.

Because it was designed for only two astronauts, the three men were overloading the canisters of lithium hydroxide that cleansed the LM of the gas. Mission control instructed Lovell to construct an adapter that would tap into the canisters of the CSM and funnel the lithium hydroxide through a tube that ran from the CSM into the LM. The adapter was a home-made affair—a canister, two tubes spliced together, and some tape—but it worked. Within an hour, carbon dioxide levels in the LM were dropping sharply, and the air in the LM was safe to breathe.

Preparing for Reentry

After being in space for more than seventy-two hours, *Apollo 13* went behind the far side of the Moon, during which time they were out of contact with mission control. Everyone in Houston waited for the next twenty-five minutes, hoping everything was okay. Finally, *Apollo 13* emerged from behind the Moon and was headed toward Earth. The lunar module's thrusters had given them the power they needed to escape the Moon's orbit and gain the push they needed to speed home.

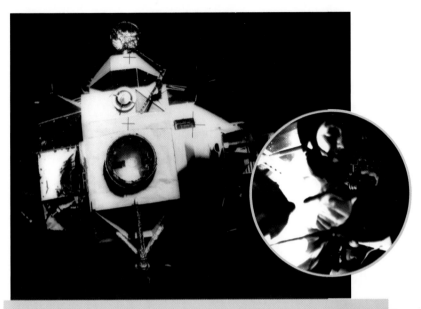

After serving as a lifeboat to the *Apollo 13* crew, the lunar module finally had to be abandoned and jettisoned just before the command module began reentry, as seen here. The inset shows James Lovell at the controls of the lunar module during the mission.

On April 16, in the early morning, Swigert began the long process of switching electrical power from the LM back to the CSM. The lunar module's batteries were being used to recharge two of the three command service module batteries. This transfer of power would take fifteen hours. The men again tried to get some rest before what

was sure to be a stressful reentry, but they were hungry, cold, and thirsty.

Drops of water continued to form on the craft's walls, windows, and instrument panels. Mission control was afraid that water could cause the controls to short-circuit or malfunction. The temperature remained barely above freezing. If it got much colder, the instruments and controls could freeze, further hurting *Apollo 13*'s chance of getting home safely.

Finally, on the morning of April 17, after four exhausting and intensely anxious days of frantic problem solving and constant worry, it was almost time to try reentry. If all went well, *Apollo 13* would be splashing down in the Pacific Ocean near Samoa around noon, and this long, drawn-out nightmare would finally be over.

Powering Up

The nightmare seemed destined to continue, however. Six and a half hours before reentry was to begin, mission control discovered that the command module's batteries did not have enough power to carry Lovell, Swigert, and Haise home. Rather than resign themselves to this grim news, however, NASA engineers worked frantically to create a new powering-up procedure that would save as much power as possible. Lovell was told not to power up the command module's systems until two and a half hours before reentry. It was thought that the batteries could provide enough power for that long.

The men climbed back into the command module and closed the hatches separating it from the service and lunar modules. Four and a half hours before reentry, *Apollo 13* was positioned into the proper angle for reentry, and then the damaged service module was jettisoned. An hour and a half before reentry, the lunar module—the trusty *Aquarius*—was also set free. Since it did not have a heat shield to protect it against the extreme heat generated during reentry, it could not make the last leg of the journey home with *Odyssey*. As the lunar module drifted away from *Odyssey*, mission control said, "Farewell, *Aquarius*. And we thank you." Lovell added, "She was a good ship" (as quoted in Jerry Woodfill's NASA article "'Houston, We've Got a Problem'").

The command module soon slid into Earth's atmosphere. The heat of reentry cut off all communications between mission control and *Apollo 13*. For three minutes, no one knew if the astronauts were safe and whether their heat shield was holding. Then, finally, Swigert's voice was heard. The entire world watched as the television showed live pictures of the capsule, floating slowly toward the water, with its three parachutes open. Against all odds, the crew of *Apollo 13* was home—and safe—at last.

A Successful—and Heroic—Failure

Though the mission had technically been a failure, NASA was still very joyful and proud with the way its astronauts and engineers triumphed over extreme difficulties. President Nixon awarded all three astronauts the Presidential Medal of Freedom. He also flew to Houston to award the honor to all the people at mission control who had helped the men return safely.

Neither Lovell, Swigert, or Haise ever flew in space again. Haise remained with NASA until

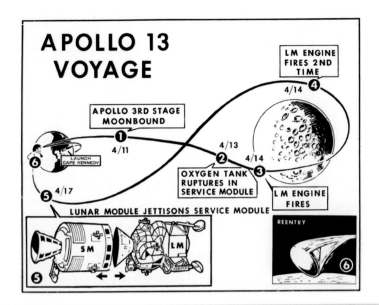

APOLLO 13 VOYAGE

LM ENGINE FIRES 2ND TIME

APOLLO 3RD STAGE MOONBOUND

4/14 ❹

❶

4/11

4/13

❷ 4/14

OXYGEN TANK RUPTURES IN SERVICE MODULE ❸

LAUNCH CAPE KENNEDY

❻

❺ 4/17

LUNAR MODULE JETTISONS SERVICE MODULE

LM ENGINE FIRES

REENTRY

SM   LM

❺

❻

This is a diagram made during the *Apollo 13* mission that indicates the time and place of the spaceflight's accident and its planned course home to safety. Insets on the diagram show how and when the service module will be jettisoned and the expected heat buildup around the Apollo capsule during reentry.

1979. He served as the backup commander for *Apollo 16* and went on to work on the space shuttle program. Swigert resigned from NASA in July 1978. In 1982, he was elected as a Colorado representative to the United States Congress. He died of cancer on December 27, 1982, however, and became the first American astronaut to die of natural causes.

Despite the near tragedy of *Apollo 13*, the Apollo program continued until the end of 1972. Each of the four remaining Apollo Moon landings was successful. Lovell and his fellow crew members would not taste this kind of success. Their dream of landing on the Moon would never be fulfilled. Yet they could take comfort in the fact that they were part of a success story equally dramatic, compelling, and heroic. As W. David Compton writes in his book *Where No Man Has Gone Before*, "By a matchless display of tenacity, resourcefulness, ingenuity, and courage, a determined group of men at mission control, working closely with a cool, expert crew, averted catastrophe and brought the astronauts through a brush with death. As an aborted mission, *Apollo 13* must officially be classed as a failure, the first in twenty-two manned flights. But, in another sense, as a brilliant demonstration of the human spirit triumphing under almost unbearable stress, it is the most successful failure in the annals of spaceflight."

A DOWN-TO-EARTH HERO

Even though his spaceflight days were over, James Lovell remained with the Apollo program, serving as a mission control adviser for *Apollo 14*. Lovell then moved on to lend his experience to the new space shuttle program. In 1971, he was named NASA's deputy director for science and applications at the Johnson Space Center in Houston. On March 1, 1973, Captain Lovell retired from both the navy and the space program.

Exploring New Worlds

In 1973, Lovell entered a whole new world—the business community. He first joined Bay-Houston Towing Company of Houston, a group involved in harbor towing, mining, and marketing of peat products for the lawn and garden industry. On March 1, 1975, he was promoted to the position of president and chief executive officer. Two years later, on January 1, 1977, Lovell accepted a position as president of Fisk Telephone Systems, Inc., also in Houston. On January 1, 1981, he was appointed group vice president of Business Communications Systems at Centel Corporation (a telecommunications company). He retired from Centel as executive vice president and member of the board of directors on January 1, 1991.

Currently, Lovell is president of Lovell Communications, a business devoted to distributing information about the United States space program. He remains a consultant to the Physical Fitness Council, a position he was appointed to in 1967 by President Lyndon B. Johnson. In this capacity, he helps the council to achieve its objective of making all citizens aware of the importance of being physically fit.

Lovell has gained an impressive share of honors, awards, and distinctions. Though there are too many to mention all of them, some of them include the Presidential Medal of Freedom, the NASA Distinguished Service Medal, two NASA Exceptional Service Medals, two Navy Distinguished Flying Crosses, and the Navy Astronaut Wings. In addition, he has received honorary doctorates from several American colleges and universities.

It is not just in outer space that James Lovell has expressed his adventurous spirit. Since his return to Earth, he has managed to travel to both the North and South Poles. Lovell made a trip to the North Pole on April 13, 1987, exactly seventeen years after his *Apollo 13* spacecraft was rocked by an explosion while on its way to the Moon. In January 2000, Lovell visited the South Pole, accompanying planetary scientist Paul Sipiera. Another astronaut, Owen Garriott, also took part in this NASA-sponsored private geological expedition near the Thiel Mountains. In the five days the team spent camping out in frigid and

windy conditions, the three-man crew found nineteen meteorites.

Lovell's New Adventures

In 1994, Lovell and Jeff Kluger authored *Lost Moon*, the story of the courageous mission of the *Apollo 13* astronauts. The next year, Lovell's book was adapted into a much-acclaimed movie called *Apollo 13*, directed by Ron Howard and starring Tom Hanks as Lovell. The thrilling movie received rave reviews and was a box-office smash. It went a long way toward reviving Americans' interest in the space program and reminding them of the true grit and can-do spirit of NASA astronauts and engineers.

In recent years, with the approval of his family, including his wife, Marilyn, and his children, Barbara, James, Susan, and Jeffrey, Lovell ventured into yet another business. In 1999, he opened Lovell's of Lake Forest, a family-style restaurant in West Lake Forest, Illinois (near Chicago). Lovell was inspired to get into the restaurant business by his older son, James, who now serves as the restaurant's executive chef.

James Lovell answers questions regarding the space shuttle *Columbia* disaster during a news conference at the Kansas Cosmosphere and Space Station in Hutchinson, Kansas, on February 3, 2003. Lovell is well qualified to speak about the dangers of spaceflight yet remains a strong supporter of manned spaceflight.

The restaurant features a $30,000 wine cellar and a plush "Captain's Quarters" filled with many items from Lovell's collection of space memorabilia. There is even a coffee table made from a map of *Apollo 13*'s proposed lunar landing site. Lovell has had the map ever since the Apollo program ended in 1972.

A True Star

In *The Last Man on the Moon*, written by Eugene Cernan and Don Davis, the authors write, "Jim Lovell is known to the world today as commander of the hard-luck *Apollo 13*. Usually happy and friendly, his leadership qualities manifested themselves at exactly the right time on that mission."

Jim Lovell is a true role model, one who has displayed great dedication to his family, his country, and his fellow humans. His life embodies the American spirit of courage, teamwork, and a search for truth and knowledge. Though he has been up in the heavens, he is a down-to-earth man who has earned an honored place in the annals of the space program. More than that, James Lovell has proved himself to be one of the most admirable and inspiring of American heroes.

GLOSSARY

capsule   A small, pressurized cabin, usually containing humans, used for spaceflight.

command service module (CSM)   The main craft on Gemini and Apollo space missions that featured two modules attached together. The command module contained the crew, spacecraft operations systems, and reentry equipment. The service module carried most of the craft's supply of oxygen, water, helium, fuel cells and fuel, and its main propulsion system.

EVA   Extra-vehicular activity; on most NASA flights, this means spacewalking. During the lunar landings of the Apollo missions, EVAs were also defined as Moon walks.

G force   The amount of force that gravity places on the body. On Earth, the force is one G. Weightlessness is zero G. During a spacecraft's

takeoff and reentry, astronauts experience about six
Gs—six times the force of gravity felt on Earth.

lunar module (LM) The craft attached to a
spacecraft's command and service modules that
detaches and ferries astronauts from the spacecraft
to the Moon and back.

Mercury space program The first manned space
missions organized by NASA, flown by the
original Mercury 7—the first group of American
astronauts in history—in single-astronaut capsules.

propulsion The action of driving something
forward with force.

rendezvous and docking Complicated
maneuvers in space that allow separate spacecraft
to draw close to each other and join together.

simulator A device that allows its user to reproduce
under test conditions the kinds of situations and
conditions likely to occur in a real-life activity.

weightlessness The floating sensation astronauts
experience when they leave Earth's field of
gravity, as if their bodies weighed nothing. The
Moon has a gravitational field one-sixth of
Earth's; astronauts aren't weightless on the
Moon, but they feel and move like they weigh
only one-sixth as much as they normally do.

FOR MORE
INFORMATION

Discovery World—The James Lovell Museum
    of Science
815 North James Lovell Street
Milwaukee, WI 53233–1426
(414) 765-9966
Web site: http://www.discoveryworld.org

Johnson Space Center
Visitors Center
1601 NASA Road 1
Houston, TX 77058
(281) 244-2100
Web site: http://www.jsc.nasa.gov

Kennedy Space Center Visitor Complex
Mail Code: XA/Public Inquiries
Kennedy Space Center, FL 32899
(321) 867-5000
Web site: http://www.ksc.nasa.gov

NASA Headquarters
Information Center
Washington, DC 20546-0001
(202) 358-0000
Web site: http://www.nasa.gov

National Air and Space Museum
Seventh Street and Independence Avenue SW
Washington, DC 20560
(202) 357-2700
Web site: http://www.nasm.si.edu

Web Sites

Due to the changing nature of Internet links, the
Rosen Publishing Group, Inc., has developed an
online list of Web sites related to the subject of this
book. This site is updated regularly. Please use this
link to access the list:

http://www.rosenlinks.com/lasb/jlov

FOR FURTHER READING

Beyer, Mark. *Crisis in Space: Apollo 13*. New York: Children's Press, 2002.

Cole, Michael D. *Apollo 13: Space Emergency*. Berkeley Heights, NJ: Enslow Publishers, Inc., 1995.

Gibson, Edward, ed. *The Greatest Adventure: Apollo 13 and Other Space Adventures by Those Who Flew Them*. Sydney, Australia: C. Pierson Publishers, 1994.

Hasday, Judy L. *The Apollo 13 Mission*. Broomall, PA: Chelsea House Publishers, 2000.

Kluger, Jeffrey, and James Lovell. *Apollo 13: Anniversary Edition*. New York: Houghton Mifflin, 2000.

Reynolds, David. *Apollo: The Epic Journey to the Moon*. New York: Harcourt, 2002.

Zelon, Helen. *The Apollo 13 Mission: Surviving an Explosion in Space*. New York: The Rosen Publishing Group, Inc., 2002.

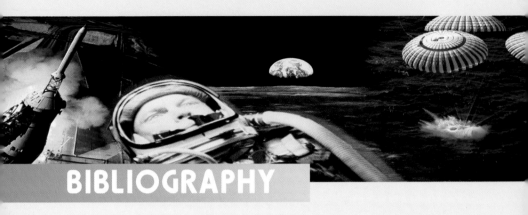

BIBLIOGRAPHY

"Apollo 8: Man Around the Moon."NASA. 2002. Retrieved June 2002(http://www.jsc.nasa.gov/er/she/apollo8.html).

Cernan, Eugene, and Don Davis. *The Last Man on the Moon: Astronaut Eugene Cernan and America's Race in Space.* New York: Griffin Trade Paperback, 2000.

Chaikin, Andrew L. *A Man on the Moon: The Voyages of the Apollo Astronauts.* New York: Viking Press, 1994.

Cooper, Henry S. F., Jr. *Thirteen: The Apollo Flight That Failed.* Baltimore: Johns Hopkins University Press, 1995.

Godwin, Robert, compiler. *Apollo 13: The NASA Mission Report.* Burlington, Ontario, Canada: Apogee Books, 2000.

Grinter, Kay, curator. "Apollo 13: 'Houston, We Have a Problem...'" NASA. April 2002. Retrieved June 2002 (http://www.pao.ksc.nasa.gov/kscpao/history/apollo/apollo-13/apollo-13.htm).

Kluger, Jeffrey, and James Lovell. *Apollo 13: Anniversary Edition*. New York: Houghton Mifflin, 2000.

Kranz, Gene. *Failure Is Not an Option: Mission Control from Mercury to Apollo 13 and Beyond*. New York: Simon & Schuster, 2000.

Sparks, Major James C. *Moon Landing, Project Apollo*. New York: Dodd, Mean & Company, 1969.

Wade, Mark. "Lovell." Astronautix.com. 2002. Retrieved June 2002. (http://www.astronautix.com/astros/lovell.htm).

Williams, Dr. David R., curator. "Detailed Chronology of Events Surrounding the Apollo 13 Accident." NASA. July 2001. Retrieved June 2002 (http://nssdc.gsfc.nasa.gov/planetary/lunar/ap13chrono.html).

Woodfill, Jerry. "'Houston, We've Got a Problem.'" NASA. April 2002. Retrieved June 2002 (http://vesuvius.jsc.nasa.gov/er/seh/13index.htm).

Zimmerman, Robert. *Genesis: The Story of Apollo 8*. New York: Four Walls Eight Windows, 1998.

INDEX

A

Aldrin, Edwin "Buzz," 45, 46, 48, 50, 51, 70, 71, 73
Apollo 8, 6, 60–69
Apollo 11, 69–74, 76
Apollo 13, 6, 7, 75–96, 99, 100, 101, 102
    crew of, 6, 75, 76, 77, 78, 79, 81, 82, 85, 86, 88, 89, 92, 93, 94, 96, 100
    problems of, 82–94
Apollo program, 23, 30–31, 35–36, 43, 44, 52, 53, 54, 56, 57, 61, 65, 69, 75, 82, 96, 97, 101
    missions of, 57–58, 59–60, 69
Aquarius, 76, 81, 86, 93
Armstrong, Neil, 70, 71, 73

B

Borman, Frank, 33, 35, 36, 38, 39–40, 41, 43, 62, 63, 64–65, 67, 68, 69

C

command module (CM), 32, 36, 38, 58–59, 61, 68, 92, 93, 94

command service module (CSM), 57, 58, 59, 60, 69, 70, 71, 73, 74, 76, 78, 81, 82, 85, 86, 88, 89, 90, 91

E

Eagle, 70, 71, 73, 74
Earth
    atmosphere of, 18, 20, 59, 62, 66, 68, 86, 88, 94
    orbit of, 6, 20, 33, 35, 36, 41, 49, 57, 59, 62, 80, 81, 88

G

Gemini 6/Gemini 6-A, 33, 35, 36–39, 41
Gemini 7, 4–6, 30, 33–35, 36–41, 62
Gemini 12, 43, 44–52, 70
Gemini Agena Target Vehicle (GATV), 45, 46, 48, 49, 50
Gemini program, 22–24, 26, 28, 30, 35, 36, 41–43, 44, 52, 53, 54
    astronauts of, 24, 25–28, 29, 30
    missions of, 28, 29, 30, 44, 70
Gerlach, Marilyn (James's wife), 12, 100
Grissom, Virgil "Gus," 28, 56, 57

H

Haise, Fred W., Jr., 76, 86, 88, 93, 94

K

Kennedy, John F., 22, 44, 53, 57, 69, 74

L

Lovell, James
awards of, 99
early life of, 8–24
family of, 12, 100
post-NASA career of, 98–101
lunar module (LM), 32, 35–36, 38, 57, 61, 69, 70, 71, 73, 76, 81, 82, 86, 87, 88, 89, 90, 91, 93

M

Mercury 4, 28
Mercury 7, the, 20, 28
Mercury program, 20, 22, 23, 26, 54
mission control/ground control, 46, 51, 54, 59, 60, 62, 63, 65, 66, 67, 71, 81, 82, 83, 85, 89, 90, 92–93, 94, 97
Moon
far side of, 6, 7, 60, 63, 64, 65, 88, 90
landings on, 6, 7, 22, 23, 32, 44, 53, 54, 56–57, 60, 61, 64, 68, 69, 70, 71–73, 74, 75, 76, 79, 85, 96, 101
missions to, 30, 33, 44, 52, 53, 54, 56–57, 63, 75
orbit of, 6, 60, 62, 66, 68, 69, 90

N

NASA (National Aeronautics and Space Administration), 4, 6, 19, 20, 22, 23, 24, 25, 33, 41, 43, 44, 45, 49, 52, 54, 46, 60, 68, 74, 76, 81, 82, 83, 89, 93, 94, 95, 97, 99, 100

O

Odyssey, 77, 81, 93

R

rendezvous and docking, 6, 30, 32, 33, 36, 39, 41, 43, 44, 45, 47, 69, 70, 74, 81

S

Saturn rockets, 58, 62, 79, 80, 81
Schirra, Walter "Wally," 33, 38, 39, 59
Shepard, Alan, 20, 22
Soviet Union, 16–17, 18, 19, 20, 22, 54–56, 60
space walks/extra-vehicular activity (EVA), 44, 45, 47, 48, 50, 51, 70
Swigert, John L., Jr., 76, 78, 81, 82, 83, 86, 88, 91, 93, 94, 95

U

United States, 8, 16–17, 18, 19, 20, 43, 45, 54, 73, 74, 75
U.S. space program, 4, 18, 20, 43, 56, 75, 97, 98, 100, 102

W

White, Edward H., 29, 30, 56, 57

About the Author

Jan Goldberg is an experienced, credentialed educator and the author of forty-seven books and hundreds of articles, textbooks, and other educational projects.

Photo Credits

Cover, pp. 1, 4–5, 27, 29, 31, 32, 33, 34, 37, 40, 42, 46, 49, 52, 55, 58, 61, 64, 65, 67, 71, 72, 77, 78, 80, 83, 84, 87, 91 courtesy of NASA, pp. 9, 10, 12, 13, 23, 101 © AP/Wide World Photos; pp. 17, 21, 95 © Bettmann/Corbis.

Designer: Les Kanturek; Editor: John Kemmerer

Only in Naples

RANDOM HOUSE / NEW YORK